Published in the UK in 1994 by
Schofield & Sims Limited, Huddersfield, England.

0 7217 5007 9

Plants

Schofield & Sims Limited Huddersfield.

Different Plants

Sequoia

Mint

Coconut palm

Olive tree

Potato

Olives

Haricot bean

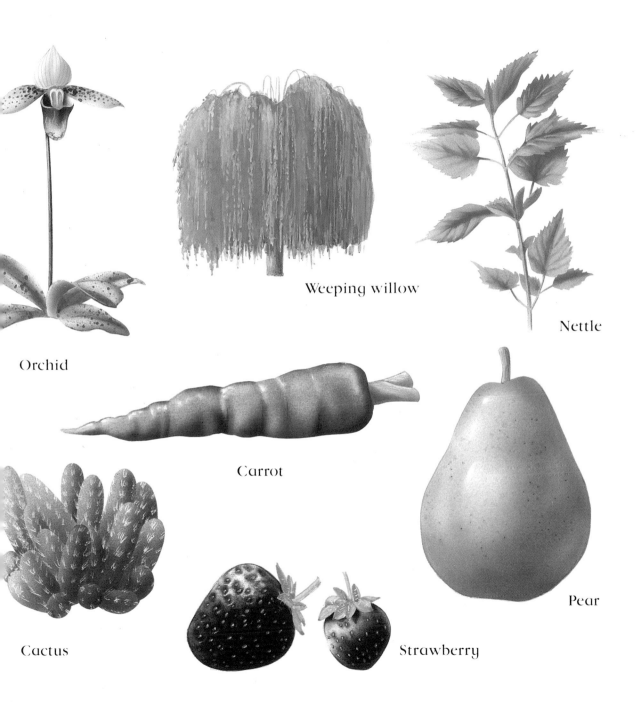

Weeping willow

Nettle

Orchid

Carrot

Cactus

Strawberry

Pear

3

Plants Around the World

Plants grow almost everywhere in the world, from the icy polar regions to the hot deserts. This is because plants can make their own food and can protect themselves from drought, wind and cold.

To survive, desert plants store water in their long roots, their thick stems or their leaves.

Many thousands of different plants grow in the tropical forests. Here, the trees grow so large that they form a kind of roof, called a canopy.

In polar regions, plants grow closely together in order to retain warmth. They remain small so that they can withstand the icy winds.

The edelweiss is covered with thick down, like fur, to shield it from the cold.

Portrait of a Plant

There are millions of plants in the world. Life exists on Earth because of plants – they produce the *oxygen* that is essential to all living things. Plants also provide us with food and drink, with clothing, and with medicine.

A plant needs air and light. It breathes and feeds itself through its leaves.

A plant also feeds itself through its roots, which anchor it in the ground and take in water and *minerals* from the soil.

Some trees, such as the horse-chestnut, have flat, smooth leaves which drop off in the autumn. These are called deciduous trees.

Other trees, such as the pine, have leaves shaped like needles which do not fall each year. These are called evergreen trees.

The Life of a Sunflower

1 – In the autumn, a sunflower seed carried by a bird or by the wind lands on the ground.

2 – This seed contains a new plant and a big enough store of nourishment to feed it until its young shoots and leaves can make their own food.

The sunflowers bloom in the summer. Bees land on the flowers and carry away with them a fine yellow dust, called pollen.

The bees then deposit the pollen on other sunflowers and fertilisation, or pollination, takes place.

6 – Leaves begin to develop.

5 – The plant becomes larger.

4 – A young shoot pushes through the ground.

3 – In spring, rain makes the seed swell. A root appears.

Fertilised flowers produce fruit and seeds, which are carried away by the wind or by animals when ripe.

The seeds will give birth to new plants.

Water Plants

The first plants to appear on Earth lived in the water. Today, most aquatic plants live in rivers, ponds and marshes. Some take root at the bottom of the water while others float on the surface. They provide shelter and food for fish and insects.

The giant water-lilies of the Amazon are so large and so thick that you could lie on top of them!

Water hyacinths float on the surface of lakes and rivers. These plants *purify* the water.

Seaweed grows in fresh or salty water. Some seaweeds are tiny, others are huge.

Some kinds of seaweed have bubbles in them so that they float. They have suckers for attaching themselves to rocks.

The Tree – a Very Special Plant

For a long, long time, people have cut down thousands of trees every year for wood. However, people today are doing their best to protect the forests, because they know that the tree is one of the Earth's most precious *resources*.

A cut is made in the trunk of the hevea tree in order to collect its sap, latex, which is used to make rubber.

Bottle corks, among other things, are made from the bark of the cork-oak tree.

The wood from trees is cut into planks to make furniture, boats, houses and musical instruments, for example.

Wood is cut into small pieces and then crushed to provide the paper pulp which is used for making books, newspapers and tissues.

13

Mushrooms

Most of the mushroom plant grows underground. The mushroom has no flowers, seeds or leaves, so it cannot make its own food. It has to feed off other plants, such as old tree stumps.

Mushrooms come in all shapes and sizes. Some of them are delicious to eat.

Others are *poisonous* and can make you very ill. Some mushrooms are deadly and can kill if eaten.

The truffle is a delicious fungus that usually grows on the roots of the oak tree. In France, people train pigs or dogs to find truffles.

Certain mushrooms grow in circles known as 'fairy rings'.

Fruits

Some fruits, such as the orange, the date and the kiwi fruit, come from far-off lands.

Redcurrants, grapes, lemon.

Cherries, apricot, plum, peach.

Vegetables

The vegetable is a plant which is grown for food. We eat certain parts of vegetables, such as the leaf, the root and the fruit.

Carrots, turnip, potatoes, onion, lettuce, cauliflower, artichoke.

Aubergine, tomatoes, peas, asparagus.

Cereals

Long ago, people grew cereals such as wheat, rice, maize and barley so that they could eat the seeds. Today, cereals are still an important food, especially for people in poor countries.

Bread is made with the white powder which is produced by grinding the ears of wheat. The powder is called flour.

The flour is mixed with a little water and yeast, and kneaded into a dough. It is then baked in an oven. Wheat is also used to make pastries and cakes.

Rice is grown in paddy-fields. It is the main food of people in Asia and parts of Africa.

Some cereals, such as oats or maize, are also used to feed animals.

Plants You Can Drink

As well as providing food for humans, plants can also be used to make drinks, such as fruit juice, wine, beer and cider.

The tea plant is a *shrub* which grows in hot countries. To obtain tea, the leaves of the plant are dried and *fermented*.

Some plants, especially herbs, can be mixed with hot water to make drinks called tisanes.

Chocolate is made with cocoa, which comes from the seeds of the cacao plant, a small tree that grows in Africa and South America.

Coffee is made from the beans of the coffee plant, which are dried and roasted and then ground into powder.

21

Spices

Spices such as pepper, cinnamon, vanilla, cloves and nutmeg come from distant lands like China and India. Long ago, spices used to be as precious as gold. People travelled across the oceans and went to war so that they could obtain spices.

Spices are used to make certain medicines, and also to make food more tasty.

The pepper plant is a climbing *shrub* which is grown in hot countries. The pepper that we use for seasoning comes from the seeds of this plant.

Vanilla comes from vanilla-pods. These scented pods are the fruit of the vanilla plant, a climbing *orchid* that grows in South America.

The bark of a young cinnamon tree is dried and made into little sticks of cinnamon.

Some Unusual Plants

The banyan, a type of fig tree, is found in Asia. A single tree can form a small forest all by itself! Roots grow on the branches of the tree and reach down to the ground. The roots start to grow in the soil and form new trees.

When it rains, the trunk of the baobab tree absorbs water and swells. When there is no rain, the tree gets thinner because it is using its reserves of water.

Some plants are meat-eaters. For example, as soon as an insect lands on the Venus fly-trap, it is caught and eaten. The plant takes two weeks to digest the insect.

The raffia is a palm tree. It has the longest leaves in the world – they can measure up to 20 metres, more than the height of some trees!

The bromeliad is the largest flower in the world. This plant is a *parasite* that lives in the jungle on the roots of certain climbing plants. Bromeliads weigh nearly 7 kilograms and have a very unpleasant smell.

In the tropical forest, certain plants grow in the hollows of tree branches. Their roots hang down from the branches so that they can absorb moisture from the air.

Glossary

Ferment
To mix products such as yeast with certain foods when they are being made. Bread dough, certain cheeses and some drinks, such as beer, are fermented.

Minerals
Elements which form the Earth's crust. Minerals are part of the composition of rocks and stones.

Orchid
A beautiful, brightly-coloured flower that often grows in tropical lands.

Oxygen
The air that we breathe contains a gas, oxygen, which is necessary for nearly all forms of life.

Parasite
An animal or a plant that lives on or in another. A parasite is harmful to its host, but does not kill it.

Poisonous
Containing a substance that can make you very ill, or even kill you.

Purify
To make clean by removing dirt and pollution.

Resource
A supply of something that can be used.

Shrub
A woody plant which is smaller than a tree and has several short stems with branches near the ground.